On
Morning
Trails

On Morning Trails

Ruth C. Ikerman

Abingdon Press

Nashville   New York

ON MORNING TRAILS

Library of Congress Cataloging in Publication Data

IKERMAN, RUTH C. On morning trails

1. Meditations I. Title.
BV4832.2.I39   242   73-18469

ISBN 0-687-28853-3

MANUFACTURED BY THE PARTHENON PRESS AT
NASHVILLE, TENNESSEE, UNITED STATES OF AMERICA

Dedicated to
my brother Bob—
Clarence Robert Percival—
with affection and appreciation

Preface

One of the joys of writing books of devotions and meditations is hearing from readers who tell how they use the material in their homes, churches, clubs, or civic groups.

Increasingly, notes have spoken of reading certain brief chapters aloud at the breakfast table as a part of morning devotions within the family circle. Such readers share the hope and promise of the ancient writer, who says in Psalm 5:3: "My voice shalt thou hear in the morning, O Lord; in the morning will I direct my prayer unto thee, and will look up."

In an effort to help us all keep looking up before beginning each day's often hectic family schedule, these short meditations have been written for use before catching a school bus, driving to work, or washing dishes.

Many of the incidents come from the walk my husband and I take each morning on the hills near our home which overlook a lovely valley and stretch away to the mountains.

May you find fresh strength for your own spiritual journey through these Bible verses, prayers, and anecdotes about the birds, flowers, trees, and sky of God's beautiful world as glimpsed on morning trails.

RUTH C. IKERMAN

Contents

1 The First Step

"He hath shewed thee, O Man, what is good, and what doth the Lord require of thee, but to do justly, and to love mercy, and to walk humbly with thy God?" Micah 6:8

The other day my mother gave me a tiny pair of white baby slippers, in which she said I had taken my first step. Holding them in my hands, I thought back to all the places that my footsteps have taken me in the busy, changing years.

The footsteps led to schools, a first job, a marriage license bureau, down a hospital corridor, to the supermarket, church on Sunday mornings, up a gangplank for travel around the world, and on countless daily errands in my own hometown.

In later years, the footsteps have included a morning walk on trails on the hilltop near our home, overlooking a valley with orange trees, and often snow-capped mountains beyond. The morning hike always proves most enjoyable, but sometimes it is not so easy to take that first step.

11

Many excuses come to mind to put off going on the trail—this is to be a very busy day with guests coming for lunch, and my husband perhaps has business appointments in town. We look at each other and wonder if we can find time for the daily walk, but we have learned that if we fail to take the walk today it will be easier to stay home tomorrow. Soon our energy level will be low, and health problems may appear.

If the first step is important in the simple act of taking a morning walk, how much greater is its importance in determining the direction a life needs for happy fulfillment. Fortunately the Bible's guidance is simplicity itself, calling upon each individual "to walk humbly with thy God."

Yet, in order to do even this, it is necessary to take the first step in determining to stay in close touch with God through daily reading of his word and through prayer and meditation.

By the process of listening for instructions from God, it is possible to receive answers to prayers, and to better each day's journey. Our footsteps today take us into many unknown areas, where problems remain to be solved, calling for new roads of peace in a time of economic change.

Daily problems cannot be solved until we take a

first step toward action, relying on God for proper guidance as to the right action. When we begin the daily walk with humility, it is possible for God's grace and goodness to help us over the rough spots on the trail.

Prayer: Dear God, help us this day to walk humbly with thee, and give us fresh visions of the joy of service with thee as our guide. AMEN.

2 Finding the Path

"Teach me thy way, O Lord; I will walk in thy truth: unite my heart to fear thy name." PSALM 86:11

How to find the path is the most important question the hiker must answer when he sets out on a walking adventure. When we decided to go for walks on our hilltop, we first asked our neighbors to suggest routes and later had the fun of personal exploration.

One of the most interesting trails proved too steep at first, until we had gained strength through trying less taxing trails. Another seemed almost monotonous as it wound through a canyon without the surprise of new vistas past a curve at the top.

After several attempts we discovered the path which seemed best for us in length, difficulty, and time involved. Then it was possible to enjoy to a greater extent the flowers along the pathway, the birds which flew overhead, and the ever-changing supply of clouds.

Something similar happens in searching for the spiritual path in life. Many of us make several attempts to find our own way through life by trails which seem to lead to mazes and complexities. Then some event causes us to pause and say, "Teach me thy way, O Lord." And, it becomes possible indeed to walk forward in truth.

Perhaps the key word in this verse asking for help is "unite," for doctors and psychiatrists feel that one of the chief problems in dealing with disturbed patients is to get them to experience a feeling of inner unity.

Today's young people express it well when they say, "Let's get it all together." Conflict often can be resolved when the heart unites to fear God and serve him in the daily walk along trails of service.

Once this feeling of unity is attained it is easier to stay on the trail and not wander off on bypaths, for unity implies a goal. The goal may be to enroll in school, contribute to funds for a church campaign, or prepare a casserole for a family night social.

The student must send for a catalog before he knows what a college requires in entrance examinations; father needs to know the extent of the family budget before the family can make contributions;

and mother may need to turn to a new recipe in her favorite cookbook.

When it is necessary to find the right trail to solve a spiritual problem, there is a map with signposts available in pertinent passages in the Bible. Sometimes looking up a word in a concordance will lead the family to new definitions of hope or fresh dimensions of love.

Prayer: Dear Father, we would find the right trail to walk this day. Give us unity of purpose and strength of heart to do thy will. AMEN.

3 Setting the Pace

"If we live in the spirit, let us also walk in the spirit." GALATIANS 5:25

There are many kinds of walks to take in this interesting world, but all have at least one factor in common—it is necessary to set a pace to get from the beginning to the end with the greatest amount of pleasure and least amount of pain.

It took a while for my husband and me to learn to pace our steps together in going over the hills. Some of the trails called for short steps up a steep incline, or longer ones on the dusty path through a small canyon.

When we had learned which pace was needed for maximum enjoyment of each distinct type of trail, we could decide easily in which direction we wanted to venture, depending on weather, time, and how we happened to feel that particular morning.

We discovered that setting the pace worked well in other activities around the house. Did we need to work at a fast pace, or could it be slower on a more leisurely day? The important thing was to learn the right pace for each task, and then move toward a destination.

One of the reasons so many good projects in churches and communities seem to falter is that the leadership fails to set the pace. Too much is expected of workers too soon, or too little is glimpsed as a possible achievement; so there is a lack of motivation to work a little harder and faster.

Yet, at whatever pace the individual decides to walk, the key factor is to "keep on keeping on" until the goal is in sight. The last few feet before the top of the hill may seem too steep to conquer, yet if they are not accomplished, the rest of the hike will have failed of its intent.

One of my friends, who accomplishes the most for many causes, told me once that all her work came from just plodding along doing a little bit each day. She organizes her time to make necessary telephone calls while she is busy in the kitchen with a pot of stew on the stove.

She has trained the children to stop by a shut-in's when they are coming from the library or headed for a school function. The result is that they are learning to be well-adjusted citizens who already keep a useful pace.

The most beautiful afghans taken to convalescent homes sometimes are formed from tiny squares, made even from scraps of yarn as knitters found time and material for a row here and a row there, never slacking their pace in thinking of others.

Setting an unselfish pace can be as much fun as learning the proper pace for an enjoyable hike in the out-of-doors.

Prayer: Father, help us match our feeble steps to thy steps of strength, that our actions may match our intentions and words. AMEN.

4 Breaking the Trail

> *"And thine ears shall hear a word behind thee, saying, This is the way, walk ye in it, when ye turn to the right hand, and when ye turn to the left."* ISAIAH 30:21

One of the best times to go for a hike is on a sunny morning after a rainstorm; even the earth seems to smell sweet, promising flowers and grasses of springtime after the storm.

There is a feeling of breaking the trail as the feet make the first imprint on the soil after the rain has washed away all evidence of past footprints. Here and there will be a tiny rivulet where the water has found a low spot and run down a miniature gully, taking with it tiny pieces of weeds, twigs, and small pebbles.

On such a morning the time has come to make a fresh start and break a trail with new footprints, even though they lead over a well-known path. A fresh sense of adventure fills the heart as the shoe makes its indentation on the moist earth.

Something of this feeling of excitement comes when anything new is tried—whether it be a plan for solving a civic problem, restoring a building, or beginning a project to build brotherhood among the community minorities.

Yet such plans sometimes falter because the pathway is not seen clearly before the leadership begins its campaign. Someone must be sure where the first steps are to be taken, and in what direction they lead.

Often human plans fail because we do not ask for divine guidance to chart a course in the right direction. This has been a normal part of human situations since Old Testament days.

Then as now, the counsel comes for the inner heart to listen quietly, waiting for the word to proceed, after first asking in prayer for help with whatever may be the current need.

Answers are available to such simple factors as to whether to turn to the right or left. Anyone who has achieved success with a dream knows that on such comparatively small factors at the beginning much depends as the project grows in magnitude.

Breaking the trail can be exciting and a consistently growing experience if a group is pointed in the right direction. One step at a time leads to victory and new horizons for future service.

Prayer: God, help us this day to listen to thy word of counsel and then to act positively, one step at a time, as we break new trails. AMEN.

5 The Scared Snake

"And they heard the voice of the Lord God walking in the garden in the cool of the day." GENESIS 3:8

Whenever friends learned that we were taking morning hikes out over the hills they were sure to ask, "But don't you see snakes?" Some added that the fear of snakes would keep them from such hiking adventures.

Of course anyone who is in the open is likely to find snakes. One is mentioned in the very first book of the Bible in connection with the experience of Adam and Eve in the Garden of Eden.

Snakes have survived along with mankind, and some experiences with snakes have been far from pleasant. We have seldom encountered them, but recall with most interest the morning when we came upon the scared snake.

He was stretched across our pathway sunning himself, and probably dreaming, for he obviously did not hear our approaching footsteps. We ourselves half thought he was a long curved branch from a nearby tree and took our stick to brush the object from the path.

At this the snake came to life and decided to get out of the way of the giants who towered over him. With a swift rushing movement he lunged forward, pulling his body across the loose dust into the brush at the side of the trail.

We stopped to look at each other and laugh as we wondered who had been more frightened, the snake or us. Glancing down at the dust, we could see plainly the pattern of his flight.

The snake had possessed the ability to move his body in such a way along the road that there was a pattern of scallops embroidering the road.

Indentations showed where he had twisted and writhed, stirring up the dirt as he slithered to the underbrush. We stood in the sunlight and studied the pattern made by his body.

Since then we have come upon such trails every once in awhile, walking the dirt road. Always we know that a snake has been there and moved on to his own projects before we arrived.

We still carry our sticks in case we are called upon to do combat; but some of our fear of snakes is gone, for we have seen how frightened the snake was as he fled from us. Often our fears look different when faced quietly.

Prayer: Father, take away our unnecessary fears, but help us to be wise in our just fears, and grow daily in courage to serve thee. AMEN.

6 A Cloud of Butterflies

> *"And I will walk among you, and will be your God, and ye shall be my people."* LEVITICUS 26:12

Once in awhile a day begins badly, and there is a let-down feeling. Why bother to take a walk out-of-doors anyway, when there is so much to do inside?

On one such occasion, we were reminded anew of the forgotten wonders of this world when we came abreast of a migratory wave of butterflies.

As we reached the crest of the hill, the first of the butterflies flew into our sight, some coming on so heedlessly that they plunged against our glasses.

Their white wings glistened in the sunlight like transparent parchment. Without the brilliant sunlight they might have been mistaken for snowflakes, each different in its beauty, yet all similar in their winged flight.

Apparently they knew exactly which way to fly, for all made a slight turn toward a tall tree and moved down into the valley creating a white gossamer scarf across the blue sky.

Endlessly they seemed to come, for this was the annual migration of these delicate creatures. We wondered how they retained the ageless memory of where to fly and when. But here was proof that they were indeed on their way from one part of the earth to another, ceaselessly pursuing their butterfly destiny.

This came as a fresh reminder that this is indeed God's world, governed by laws of which many of us are at most times unaware. We see a lone butterfly and dismiss it casually from our minds unless it is of particular beauty in colors which appeal to us.

Yet butterflies by the millions are a part of the ecology of the earth, pursuing their necessary part in its economy. By some inner rhythm they know when to move from the cold climate to the warm when the seasons swing into action.

Along the way they are nourished and sustained for their journey. Watching their delicate wings beating so sturdily through the sky as they continued their long flight, my husband and I felt a fresh surge of humility.

Who are we to dare to forget that God has promised since Old Testament times, "And I will walk among you, and will be your God, and ye shall be my people"?

This is a privilege not to be overlooked as we turn to the often routine and mundane tasks of each day. If we are children of God then we can ask him for help, and be assured of his guidance in our most strenuous journeys with even fragile human strength.

Prayer: God of beauty, accept our thanks for the butterflies of life, and sustain our weak wills so we may fly to our tasks with strength. AMEN.

7 The Blossoming Pink Tree

"For his anger endureth but a moment; in his favour is life: weeping may endure for a night, but joy cometh in the morning." PSALM 30:5

All winter the landscape looked so bare it was as if God himself were angry at the hills. Gray days kept even the shadow of green from showing through, and the trees were like skeletons.

Illness kept us indoors for a week or so, and then one misty morning we started out over the hills again. Suddenly we stopped still in our tracks, for over the next rise was a glimpse of pink—rosy as a vagrant cloud at sunrise.

What could it be? Surely not the old gray tree which had seemed ready to be discarded and unlikely ever to bloom again. But the abundance of dark, wet days had brought the tree back to life.

Ahead of us were dainty pink blossoms arranged so profusely on the old gray limb that they seemed like a frilly pink parasol opened to keep off the mists.

Surely in its youth the tree could not have been more beautiful than it was now in old age, its gnarled limbs looking stiff and arthritic, but still pointing toward the sky.

We walked up toward the pink blossoms and the gray limbs silhouetted against the hillside and saw that there was a patch of blue sky shining through the dismal day.

While we watched, the sun came out, making the mist on the tree sparkle like sequins on a pink party dress. What a beautiful sight was the blossoming pink tree, well worth waiting for in a long series of routine walks past the gray tree.

Sometimes this sudden beauty can appear in life also. We think a child will never get over his stubbornness, and then he becomes the most willing worker in his Scout troop.

An older friend who has been melancholy and emotional in daily telephone calls somehow gets a fresh grip on life, and prepares a tasty supper for guests, or volunteers to serve on a committee.

When life itself becomes so dull through its being so very daily, it is easy to think that its surprises are gone. This is a fallacy and should be fought with hopefulness, for if we wait long enough surprises of beauty lie ahead.

Often we ourselves must become a part of life's surprises, using initiative in preparing a treat for an invalid or telephoning an old friend who has been neglected in the rush of routine.

The tree along the trail reminds that God always plans for joyous mornings ahead, and we must be alert to find and accept such beauty, like the blossoming pink tree.

Prayer: God, keep us aware of loveliness even when it is temporarily hidden from our eyes, and help our own lives become more lovely. AMEN.

8 Tracks in the Snow

"Blessed is every one that feareth the Lord; that walketh in his ways."
PSALM 128:1

Snowfall in our area is relatively rare, so when it does occur the occasion is reason enough for an extra walk. White petals of snow hang from the bushes like dainty blossoms heralding a new season. What they lack in fragrance, they make up in their delicate fragile beauty.

There is something about the snow which must be enjoyed this very moment, for it is likely to melt when the sun shines and disappear into the ground when the weather becomes warmer. An air of mystery usually surrounds snow except where its abundance makes it monotonous before the season ends.

On one brilliant morning when we set out to enjoy the snow which had fallen during the night, we found we had been preceded by a variety of unseen friends of the hilltop. Their tracks were already in the clean snow, urging us onward.

Here were the tracks of birds and a round spot in the middle of the track where a bunny had sat down to look over the landscape.

The bird tracks with three-pointed prongs seemed to go in circles before moving from the trail into the underbrush. Had they been playing with one another before going away in search of food?

The speed with which the rabbit had moved was apparent by the way the tracks were spaced further apart as he had jumped a little further each time down the trail. Was the neighbor's dog perhaps chasing him at this point?

It was fun trying to fathom what had gone on in the fresh snow before our arrival, and on the return trip we could see plainly our own footsteps.

The outline of our hiking shoes showed clearly in the snow, long strides indicating our purposeful walk to a predetermined point. The extra steps taken to get the best view at a panoramic spot were clearly etched in the snow, and we remembered how we had stopped to talk and point to the snow-capped peaks beyond.

Not often do we have the chance to see exactly

where our footsteps have taken us on any walk as we did that day in the snow. Yet the steps we take add up to infinity and form the pattern of our lives, whether we see them or not.

Fortunately we have the promise of blessing for those who fear the Lord and who try to walk in his way.

Prayer: God, help us this day to direct our footsteps aright so that we do not need to wish to erase them at journey's end. AMEN.

9 Sounds Above the Trail

"Blessed is the people that know the joyful sound: they shall walk, O Lord, in the light of thy countenance." PSALM 89:15

The sounds of birds accompany us on many of our morning walks, at times sounding more joyful than at others, but always with a happy chorus of trills and answering notes from their own bird friends.

Hearing the birds sing their special songs adds to the delight of any morning walk, for there is something contagious about their joyousness.

If we start out in a grumpy mood, the sound of the birds penetrates into our moodiness until our hearts automatically become lighter and begin to shed some of the routine load.

At first glance it is hard to see why the birds sound so joyous, for they are about their daily task of finding food for themselves and their families. Yet they take time to sing as they go through the routine of flying over the ground, eyes alert to kernels of grain or an unsuspecting insect.

As a part of the natural world, they emphasize God's intent for this to be a joyous experience for his children, for the Bible reminds that the people who know "the joyful sound" are indeed blessed.

What are some of the joyful sounds of life? The giggle of a young child just learning to dress himself when he finds he can tie his own shoes, the laughter of an older brother scuffing with a playmate on the lawn, or the singing of a teen-aged girl when she is unobserved at her clean-up tasks in her room.

As we grow older, sometimes it is the memory of a joyous sound which can comfort most in trying to adjust to a loss. Hearing the remembered inflection of a loved one's voice in a simple phrase of advice can bring fresh courage to reshoulder the burden of a new day in a changed year.

Joyous sounds are to be cultivated, for they give harmony to living. They are needed to counteract the words of criticism, so often given even by those we love, which tend to destroy confidence and break down energy into worry.

Every once in awhile it is a good idea to take a

straight look at our individual conduct and see whether it adds to life's joyousness or to its dreary, ordinary perplexities.

Turning to the radio or a stereo to find some lilting music can often help change a mood of fearfulness or somberness into one of joyful activity as we move through the day.

Prayer: Father, we truly want to walk in the light of thy countenance and hear the joyful sounds of life. Help us this day. AMEN.

10 The Delicate Survivor

"And thine age shall be dearer than the noonday; thou shalt shine forth, thou shalt be as the morning." JOB 11:17

At the very end of the point where we survey the valley on our morning walks, there is a rough promontory which seems an unlikely place for a flower to bloom. Yet, often at our feet are tiny delicate pinkish-purple flowers, and we have come to look for the first one as a harbinger of springtime.

At first glance the tiny flower seems just a dot of pink against a stone, or perhaps a little round insect lodging on the dust. When we peer closer, we see five petals so transparent you can almost see the blue sky through them when held up to the morning sunlight.

Smaller than a penny in size, the flower is perfectly formed in all its petals and yellow center. It has surprising strength, for if we pick one and carry it carefully in our hands all the way home, it will float in a dish for several days before withering away.

As we pass the little blue saucer on our way through the house on various chores, we take a glance at the tiny flower which looks so cheerful and jaunty floating alone on the miniature lake.

How the flower could survive and grow out-of-doors with such handicaps of earth and rock is just the first part of the blossoming miracle, for it lives indoors as well.

Sometimes people are like this tiny flower. We have elderly friends who have seen much hardship and lived through it in spite of diminishing, never robust, physical strength.

Indeed, as they come to the twilight years of life they seem to have more endurance for sorrow and suffering than do many of their younger friends who inherently have more of what is usually considered life's blessing of strength and energy.

Always it is a joy to see the elderly friends who have survived with fortitude, and who have at the same time managed to keep a certain fragile air of hope and a delicate preoccupation with dreams for a happy future.

They are as refreshing to friends of all ages as the flower which pushes its way through the rocky soil to show its loveliness and strength as the delicate survivor.

Prayer: God, give each of us the power to endure so that the end of life may be blessed with the beauty of life's morning. AMEN.

11 Misty on the Moors

"My soul waiteth for the Lord more than they that watch for the morning: I say, more than they that watch for the morning." PSALM 130:6

Occasionally in our land of sunshine there will come a morning so misty with clouds foreshadowing rain, that it seems we can hardly see the ground beneath our feet.

Shall we try to take the morning walk when it is misty on the moors? Or shall we wait for a better day, then how long must we wait?

No longer do we let the misty mornings of heavy clouds keep us from getting out on the trail, for we have learned that such gray days bring their own beauty.

There is a softness in the atmosphere which seems to brush the cheek with a special caress, as if the hand of God were reaching out through the mist to touch his children.

Sometimes a drop of moisture will gather on a

41

pair of glasses or an eyebrow, and we brush it aside the better to see the trail, and it seems almost as one of nature's teardrops.

On rare mornings the mist will be so thick that we cannot make out the bushes at the side of the trail, walking along by the feel of the cleared hard dirt beneath our feet.

Then, the first fading of the mist will begin, and we can make out a clump of sage, a twist of mesquite, or the next rise in the path, a tiny hill ahead.

As such dull sunlight filters through the mist it makes ghostly shadows, not at all like the usual picture—something to stir the imagination deciding what the trees resemble.

Always such mornings are reminiscent of happy hours of travel on the low hills and moors of Yorkshire in England, leading up to Scotland with its heather.

In travel, such traditional weather and sights are a part of the charm, and yet when the mists come closer to home we often sigh and wish for the more average day when things appear normal.

So it is that in life we are almost afraid of the misty days when we cannot see clearly what lies ahead. Perhaps it means we must wait for a signal

42

from someone else—the report of the doctor, the results of the school examination.

Meanwhile, life itself seems misty, and the plans we have made are hidden in gloom. Keeping as close to our schedule as possible in spite of uncertainties is one way of making progress toward our dreams. Through the mist the face of God may be faintly hidden, but soon will appear in all its loving kindness.

Prayer: God, we would draw closer to thee as we wait for the mists to lift. Show us thy path of service. AMEN.

12 Guardian Angels

*"And he said unto me, The Lord be-
fore whom I walk, will send his angel
with thee, and prosper thy way."*
GENESIS 24:40

Walking through the Southwest and glancing at
the sometimes barren hills, hikers frequently are
told that there is an angel on the hills.

Sure enough there will be a white outcropping
of rock which seems to be a figure with arms out-
stretched. Some of these imaginative forms are
quite impressive, and others take a closer watching
to discover any resemblance to the form of an
angel. By using a pair of field glasses, it may be
possible to bring the rock into better focus and
see an angel figurine.

In our homes we place a ceramic birthday angel
of the month, or the angel with a measuring spoon
in hand to help in the kitchen. Yet the angel which
counts is the one the hiker carries with him in
his heart, a feeling of oneness with his Creator, and

44

a reliance on his goodness for guidance on the daily walk of duties, burdens, and pleasures.

Perhaps in a simpler age, it was easier for people to believe that guardian angels accompanied them through life than in this time of skepticism.

Yet modern hikers who have survived periods of being lost in a forest or desert often refer to "my guardian angel." Some even say that when they grew quiet enough they felt the actual presence of someone close to them, keeping watch over them and giving strength.

Certainly the Old Testament promise concerning the angel and its presence has come true for many when they have been in need of such help and have asked for it.

What was the purpose of the guardian angel? The Bible says to "prosper thy way," another proof of the intention of God that his children should live abundant lives.

A second clause joins this promise, for the angel's power comes from "the Lord before whom I walk." Again, the emphasis is on the walk, but it is also important to know whom to follow.

When the glory is gone out of daily living, and the heart is overwhelmed and lonely, there is power in turning to the guardian angels of the trail.

This involves first a new resolve to follow God in life's daily walk, and confidently to expect that his angels will prosper the way of the seeking heart, walking in faith.

Prayer: Dear God, we thank thee for the times when thy guardian angels have helped us over rough places on the trail. Help us now. AMEN.

13 In Sunshine and Shadow

"Then spake Jesus again unto them, saying, I am the light of the world: he that followeth me shall not walk in darkness, but shall have the light of life." JOHN 8:12

When we are asked if we get tired of hiking the same trail each morning, my husband and I look at each other and smile. Early we learned the secret that the same trail never looks quite the same in any two days because of the sunshine and the shadows.

One morning the light will shine brightly on every indentation clearly defined before us, and the rays will glisten upon the sage bushes and the chapparal.

The next morning may seem the same, but the sun will be at a slightly different angle if we leave just fifteen minutes later, making a noticeable difference in the pattern of the leaves on the dusty trail as silhouettes of beauty.

Then there will come a morning of such deep shadows that the surrounding landscape seems a gray blur, and sometimes it will be completely obliterated by fog or mist.

Whether in sunshine or shadow, the trail has its own special attractions to lead us on day after day, to take the necessary walk prescribed for good health, which adds to life's zest and enjoyment.

What we have learned further is that during the hour of the walk the sunshine and shadows change, for life does not ever stand still, even though we fall into the habit of thinking that it does.

A passing cloud will make a shadow of deeper blue on the hills, and when it has moved on, the light blue-gray of the mountain range will once again appear in unbroken beauty.

A dark cloud may come down from the sky covering the highest peak where it may be snowing but on the ground the sunlight slants with its familiar patterns of beauty. How different the same trail looks in sunshine and shadow, though it essentially is the same trail.

We do not have to walk in darkness if we remember that beyond the shadows is the true and eternal light, available to each of us. With this confidence, we can walk through the shadows doing our best because we await the coming light.

Prayer: God, whether this day holds more sunshine or shadow we cannot know at this point, but we thank thee for the promise of light. AMEN.

14 The Bird in the Yucca

"Ye shall walk after the Lord your God, and fear him, and keep his commandments and obey his voice, and ye shall serve him, and cleave unto him. DEUTERONOMY 13:4

A tall stalk of creamy white yucca is one of the landmarks on our daily walk. In springtime the ungainly upshoot is covered with myriads of individual blossoms, the rich creamy shade being tinged with a light lavender when examined closely.

Sometimes a bee comes buzzing out of the yucca bell or a tiny moth flies away, proof of the plant and insect ecology, where all life unites in propagation and mutual care in their world.

We love the yucca for still another reason; it is the home of one of our favorite birds, but whether he uses it as a beach home or mountain home we have never been able to decide.

Part of the year our bird lives in this yucca plant, but he has a second home just over the hill in a tree in another valley. When we first encountered him, he was afraid of us and would fly speedily from one home to the other when he saw us coming down the trail.

Now that he is used to us on the morning walk, the bird calmly stays by the yucca plant, looking us over as intently as we do him, trying to see his feathers in all their perfect array.

He permits us to stop and listen to his song, and once in awhile will put on a special acrobatic act for our benefit. This involves jumping up from the yucca and with one graceful motion catching the insects he sees flying through the air.

Our eyes do not see them, but the eyes of the bird are intent on what has been provided for his food. With a quick movement of his wings he leaves the yucca and flies straight upward, pauses momentarily in midair, and comes back down to enjoy his special morsel of food.

If there are many insects in the air, we can watch undisturbed for as long as we choose while he continues to entertain. Seeing the perfomance is a humbling experience, proving again the marvelous ways in which God provides for all his creatures, even the bird on the yucca.

Instinctively the bird seems to know the right

way to find his food. We return resolved to try to accept with gratitude the blessings prepared for us and to seek them diligently.

The Bible's advice is explicit; we are to walk, fear, obey, serve, and cleave as God's plan unfolds for our lives.

Prayer: God, give us the grace we need to trust thee more, and to know that our daily needs will be provided by thee. AMEN.

15 Greening Out Above the Gray

> *"Though I walk in the midst of trouble, thou wilt revive me: Thou shalt stretch forth thine hand against the wrath of mine enemies, and thy right hand shall save me."* PSALM 138:7

The gray bush alongside the trail seemed completely dead. Its limbs were brittle, and there had been no leaves at all in the past two seasons.

Then came the winter of heavy rains, and we would not have been surprised if this bush had been toppled over and swept away. We kept neglecting to pull it out as we walked past, perhaps because there was a certain dignity and wry beauty in the gray limbs, even in their apparently dying stages.

Then one morning when we paused to take a good look at the gray bush, we were startled to find that green was appearing on the top of the dry skeleton. Putting our fingers to the tiny limbs, which in former times had broken off as brittle

53

refuse at the slightest touch, we found that the rain was softening and fattening the branches.

It was true, then, that the green was coming from a new upsurge of strength within the plant, and it was not just a lichen growing on bare wood.

Each morning that we glanced at the gray plant it seemed a little greener than the day before. We called it the green-haired bush, for indeed the bushy green at the top seemed to be a masquerade wig above a gray ghost costume.

Gradually, new short branches appeared at the sides, each a lovely green. Our dried-up bush soon was one of the most interesting parts of the morning jaunt as we studied its fresh progress.

Here was proof again that no matter how troubled the situation may have been, or how impossible it looks to the outside, there is power within when strong life-giving sources can reach the disabled.

Often individuals feel so troubled that it seems there is no hope of revival, but all nature offers proof that new health and strength can come to even the most hopeless cases. The important thing is to stay where life-giving energy can get to the root of the problem and help rejuvenate the heart, mind, and emotions.

This can never happen if the individual gives up in despair. Just staying on the pathway of life often calls for courage, but so long as the individual remains at his task, there is the chance of greener days, progress, and success.

Prayer: God, keep us from desolation, and revive us with new showers of blessing that we may yet achieve our intended destiny. Amen.

16 The Ground Around You

"Then said the Lord to him, Put off thy shoes from thy feet: for the place where thou standest is holy ground."
ACTS 7:33

When the family is away on a vacation, it is easier to find interesting places to walk than at home, or so it usually seems. In fact it took us quite a while to discover the advantages of the hike closest to our home.

Why should it be that we always think it will be more fun to walk on mountain trails many miles from where we live? Is it true that the sands of far-removed beaches have more exotic appeal than those closer to us?

All of us have tinges of envy in our spirit and think that the grass is greener on the other side of the trail. Yet by failing to walk on the paths closer to us, we limit our strength and are not prepared for fullest enjoyment of more distant trails if they come into our lives.

It was necessary in biblical times to remind the faithful that the "place where thou standest is holy ground." This verse in the New Testament is repeated from an earlier verse in the Old Testament, showing how little human nature had changed in the intervening years.

The advice rings true today. If exciting trails are not available, there is the opportunity to find excitement in the ordinary trail. One way to do this is to look at the familiar surroundings with new eyes.

A friend who could no longer walk because of a physical handicap refused to be intimidated by her wheelchair surroundings. She bought a pair of binoculars and brought the trail to her chair.

One day she showed me a bird's nest, and another day pointed the glasses to the grass where she had discovered busy ants carrying food to their hill.

The glasses showed her fresh beauty in the nearby rose, and made it possible for her to examine closely the leaves which fell from the over-arching tree.

If this fresh look from limited circumstances can add to life's enjoyment in discouraging circumstances, think how much more joy can be found in the ordinary day with its average duties when one remembers to consider such tasks as holy.

The walk through the kitchen or down a business corridor can become a close walk with God when the attitude of the heart is that all ground is holy, to be treated with reverence.

Prayer: God, forgive us for being disenchanted with the places thou dost give us in life. Restore to us a sense of holiness and wholeness. AMEN.

17 Lightning Lizards

> *"Yea, he sent out his arrows, and scattered them; and he shot out lightnings, and discomfited them."*
> PSALM 18:14

When we asked a newcomer in our area to join us on our walk, she replied, "I'd love to go if you promise to keep the lizards off the path."

Apparently they "discomfited" her and made her want to flee, as the ancient word suggests. We could not agree to keep the lizards away, for they dash like arrows with lightning speed across the dusty trail.

Our philosophy is that the lizards lived along the trail long before we arrived here, and their numerous progeny probably will be there long after we are gone, so meanwhile why not enjoy the lizards?

They dart with such swiftness on the path that it is hard to see their coloration which is often a dusty gray or an earth brown, or perhaps almost black like some of the nearby boulders.

Sometimes we think they follow us home from the trail for we see new sizes of lizards sunning themselves on the rock wall which lines the driveway near our home.

On certain sunny mornings the lizards seem to engage in acrobatics as they lift themselves on their short but strong legs, and let themselves down till their stomachs touch the warm stones.

If they see human feet approaching, they dart like lightning into the underbrush. When we go out for the beginning of the hike, we may hear a soft rustle in the leaves near the hedge telling us that the lizards are watching our departure.

On return they may be sunning themselves on the doormat sorry to see us back, for they scurry away to hide as we put our walking poles by the door and reach for the key.

We always call them the lightning lizards, and we did not know how apt this phrase was until a young friend watched with us one afternoon during a sudden thunderstorm.

As we listened to the deep thunder and waited for the next bright flash of light to break the skies into pieces, our visitor said, "That lightning sure looks like your yellow lizards."

True enough, the streaks of light across the

stormy sky were much like our scurrying friends of the trail. Such demonstrations of speed and power speak of the God back of the universe who provides infinite diversity within the sameness of familiar images.

Prayer: God, we thank thee for all evidences of thy greatness as creator, in land and sky, as we share thy world of wonders. AMEN.

18 Push the World Behind

"And in the fourth watch of the night Jesus went unto them, walking on the sea." MATTHEW 14:25

Ahead of us on the trail was a puddle of water reflecting the blue of the sky in the sunshine following rain. At first glance it seemed that a little bird was actually walking on the water, but as we came closer the bird took to its wings in flight.

We could see the long legs like stilts, which identified it as a sandpiper, which sometimes strays inland to our area to enjoy the irrigation canals. With its tall thin legs it had been wading as we walked the trail.

There is something about our land-locked feet which makes us long to move on the water or in the sky. The development of water skis has gone a long way toward helping young people today get the feel of walking on water. Now there are attempts at wings to enable people to go through the air.

All such attempts seem to tie in with one of the philosophical aims of walking, which is to push the world behind. Often the world is far too much with us, and we want to get away from it all, so we begin by taking a little walk.

When earthbound trails become routine, we long for faith to conquer walking in the sky and on the water. Meanwhile, there are other paths to walk which call for a great deal of faith and bring fresh adventures into our lives.

These are the new paths of service, brought to the mind and heart by human needs. A friend became aware of the opportunity to help minority children learn art forms and volunteered her services. She said to me, "I feel as though I were walking on water, it is all so new and untried a field for me, but very exciting."

She persisted in going each week to meet with her young pupils, many from homes poor in material advantages. At first they did not know how to hold crayons or paint brushes. So she started with finger painting, just a soft substance they could smear on paper into designs which expressed their dreams, and often revealed their hostilities.

She began to ask her friends for contributions so she could buy canvas for the older pupils, and we all shared her joy when a lad won an art prize for his gaily colored poster.

The beginning of her new project had called for faith to walk a new path. Always it takes faith to walk on the waters of our lifetime and learn to push the world behind us.

Prayer: God, we reach out for more and ask thee to help us achieve our full potential that we may better serve others and thee. AMEN.

19 Footprints

> *"That thou mayest walk in the way of good men, and keep the paths of the righteous."* PROVERBS 2:20

Apparently another hiker had been wearing sandals with an unusual crisscross design on the sole, for we could follow his footprints easily as we walked along the familiar trail.

His daily schedule started earlier than ours, we decided, and speculated who took this route at such an early hour. It was a couple of weeks before we came face to face with the owner of the shoes who proved to be a neighbor, and became a good friend.

We told him we had been walking in his footprints, and we laughed together thinking how he might have led us astray had he veered from the beaten path.

There is a certain fascination in footprints. A baby's first footsteps constitute one of the most remarkable experiences of his entire life, say doctors and psychiatrists.

Life after learning to walk is different, when the child can be in an upright position and explore cabinets and cupboards, bookcases and low tables. Footprints often mark the beginning of discipline problems.

Life constantly calls us onward to make new footprints in untried ventures. This is a personal challenge as well as one with national and international consequences.

Certainly one of the most memorable pictures of the space age for generations to come will be the footprints made on the moon by the first explorers to arrive from earth. After the astronauts had moved on, their footprints remained, captured forever on film. Families watched together while the film was run and rerun on television.

Footprints on the moon appear in numerous illustrations of the printed words about the astronauts' voyages into space. They are a visual reminder of the footprints of those who have gone ahead to prepare the way.

Footprints do matter in life. It is always important to see that our footprints are headed in the direction of worthy goals, and the way the individual truly wishes to go. Meanwhile, neighbors, friends, or family may be following closely in our footprints along life's daily pathway.

Prayer: God, we would keep to the roadway of righteousness in spite of temptations and daily busyness. Help us to walk aright. AMEN.

20 Remember to Look Up

> *"For the Lord God is a sun and shield: the Lord will give grace and glory: no good thing will he withhold from them that walk uprightly."*
> PSALM 84:11

What was that sound we were hearing as we walked along? It baffled us as we scuffed against the brown leaves. Then as we looked up, the mystery became clear.

We could see leaves falling to the ground. What we were hearing was the stealthy sound of the leaves as they walked softly across the sidewalk on a sunny, windswept day in late summer.

On another morning, there was a haunting sound like a train blowing in the distance, or the echo of a ship's horn at sea. It sounded so distant we thought we might be hearing it only in memory, then we remembered to look upward.

High above us in the bright morning sky was a thin, V-shaped, bevy of birds winging their way southward. We were hearing the wild geese crying on their way from the cold climate to the warmer, following their God-given instincts.

How much beauty we would have missed if we had not remembered to look up. Often we can find the source of our comfort and strength by looking up from our daily tasks, which far too often keep our eyes riveted to the ground.

We fear to look up toward the sun, for we have been trained since childhood to avoid its direct rays. One of the first requisites for hiking seems to be a pair of dark glasses as a shield from the sun's rays.

But the Bible says that "the Lord God is a sun and shield," providing both the light and the protection for those who look up to him. Primitive man who worshiped the sun held this ball of fire in great fear, but man today can worship God in faith.

The promise further is that "the Lord will give grace and glory," and will withhold nothing "from them that walk uprightly."

This type of walk calls for a daily attempt at righteousness in dealing with neighbors and friends. It may mean refusing to repeat a story of gossip, or taking the initiative in defending the one whom others are linking with scandal.

Walking uprightly calls for keeping on when the way is rough, though it would be much easier to stop and not try to move forward.

Above all, the walk in righteousness calls for looking up. This may take just a moment from the straightforward walk into service, but it can make the difference between dullness and beauty.

Prayer: Father, keep us mindful of thee and thy love for us as we look upward from our tasks that we may return to them strengthened. AMEN.

21 A Handful of Pebbles

> *"Among the smooth stones of the stream is thy portion; . . . Should I receive comfort in these?"* ISAIAH 57:6

As our morning walks progressed, our interest grew in the pebbles and stones found along the pathway. At first they all looked alike, and we gave them scant notice.

Then one morning the sun glinted off a plain rock until it looked like dazzling gold, and we stooped down to pick it up and examine it more closely. Sure enough, it seemed to have gold particles.

This prompted a telephone call to a friend who is somewhat of an amateur geologist, and he explained the composition of this rock to us, and suggested a simple book for us to use.

This led to picking up more rocks and trying to identify them after returning home. Another friend told us to look for those rocks which could be cut

71

and polished and invited us to see her collection of stones.

By polishing the stones, she had produced beautiful gems, some suitable for placing in brooches and rings. The equipment necessary was comparatively simple, but she said, "It takes a long time to produce the shine."

This is a fascinating hobby for many during retirement years, or for those recovering from illness. The answer to boredom and monotony may lie in discovering the hidden beauty of pebbles.

The stony disappointments of the heart also may have unexpected centers of beauty and understanding.

But the polishing of life takes a long, long time. Often time itself is the only healing agent after meeting a rocky discouragement that seems too much for the soul to handle.

Friends may try to help, many family members may offer sympathy, but the stone remains, until time has polished away the rough edges.

The way the waiting time is spent makes a difference in the smoothing of the stones. If the mind is directed inward to the individual's problem, the stone seems heavier than ever. Once the first indication of interest in others occurs, the stone becomes easier to carry.

Seeing a collection of pebbles brought back from our trips brings to mind the pebbles of the heart, and the blessing of time in turning hardships into lovely gems of happy memories.

Prayer: God, give us the comfort we need this day, and lighten our stony hearts that they may show forth thy beauty. AMEN.

22 Call of the Coyotes

"For the Lord thy God walketh in the midst of thy camp, to deliver thee, and to give up thine enemies before thee." DEUTERONOMY 23:14

The first time the call of the coyotes is heard over the trail is a memorable experience for any hiker. There is loneliness in the haunting call, particularly since the coyote is an elusive animal not often seen at the time of his call.

In fact, the coyote call comes most poignantly on the nights of a full moon, when it seems that several of them have come together to bark at the moon with their mournful voices.

From out in the area of the trails of our morning walks, my husband and I would hear the coyotes call on moonlit nights. Their chorus would wake us and sometimes sound so close that we would look out the windows to see if we could discover any of the large, wild dogs of the trail.

They kept to their hidden places of congregation

74

on the trail as the echo of their voices came through the windows of our home, making us glad of each other's companionship. In their plaintive call was something of the forlorn sound of a train in the night, calling to distant places and times.

Perhaps the coyote call speaks in some unforgettable way to the kinship of all of God's creatures in their essential loneliness, until they find their rightful places in his world.

With only the sound of the coyote and pictures from books to identify the animal, we hardly expected to recognize one immediately if we should encounter it on the trail. When the moment arrived on the sunlit path, the coyote was more surprised than we.

Usually most wary, the animal apparently was intent on something else, for we had come quite close when it suddenly stopped in its tracks. Gracefully it lifted its head with the pointed nose and stared at us with beady eyes.

We stopped also and stared back, glad for this moment of introduction to the animal which had called to us through the lonely night. Satisfied in curiosity, the coyote turned abruptly and left us, trotting off with both speed and dignity.

We lost him as he took to the underbrush, so we

could not tell whether his lair was close by the trail or over the next hill.

Now when he sings at night, we visualize him and think of our new friend on the trail, living his life of ancient knowledge in these days of modern loneliness.

Prayer: Dear God, keep us in tune with thy calls upon our hearts. We are grateful for thy walk with us in the midst of our days. AMEN.

23 Falling Feathers

"He shall cover thee with his feathers, and under his wings shalt thou trust: his truth shall be thy shield and buckler." PSALM 91:4

Walking the trail one sunlit morning, we were startled by something falling across our path, touching our faces with a light caress similar to a snowflake.

Without any sign of a storm, what could have caused this sudden contact? Brushing away the surprising intruder from above, we found it to be a soft feather falling from the wing of a passing bird.

We stooped to pick it up, and looked at it carefully in our hands. What seemed at first merely a gray feather turned out to have an outer edge of white and inner lines of black.

We carried it home and put it under a microscope. What appeared as just a plain gray feather was indeed a picture of almost indescribable loveliness.

Such a pattern of beauty could not be discarded, so we placed the fallen feather in a tiny ceramic vase we had brought from a trip to Mexico. Its brown clay had a miniature rose painted on the side with a forget-me-not blossom.

In this earthy vase, the feather reminded of courageous flight through blue skies, and it was pleasant on the kitchen windowsill. Soon it was joined by another feather we found on a later trip.

Once aware of feathers, we began to collect them and were amazed at their differences as well as their lovely symmetry. Soon it was necessary to get a larger vase, this time a soft blue one made by a young artist friend.

For a season, the bouquet of feathers blossomed as gaily as did the flowers in our garden. Each time we passed the vase with its unusual array, we were reminded of the beauty of feathers, which before we had taken for granted.

There was new meaning in an old familiar verse from the psalms, for when God "shall cover thee with his feathers," he is using a cloak of great softness and warmth.

Not for his children is a harsh covering, but the sweetness of a father's caress with loving arms. We do not have to be afraid when there is such gentleness, for "under his wings" we may trust.

It was a good morning when the falling feathers reminded us of another of God's blessings along life's trail.

Prayer: Father, all of us need thy love and thy benediction. Cover us now with thy feathers of kindness, as we trust thy wings. AMEN.

24 Blue Lupine Carpet

"The flowers appear on the earth; the time of the singing of birds is come, and the voice of the turtle is heard in our land." SONG OF SOLOMON 2:12

Probably the happiest time of year for a good walk is the springtime. Nothing heralds this so completely, in many parts of the world, as the appearance of the carpet of blue lupine.

Just as the blue flowers come to the brown earth of our hilltop, so they appear in many countries where we have traveled. A hardy member of the sweet pea family, the lupine adjusts itself wherever it is geographically placed.

Where the soil is abundant and rich, the lupine may grow to quite a height, and where the earth is rocky and sparse, the plant will be quite small, hugging the ground.

Even the shade of blue seems to vary according to the type of lupine as if governed also by the amount of minerals in the soil, for it may appear a dark, rich, blue, a periwinkle, or just plain blue.

The flowers always appear sturdy and grow steady like the plumage of a prince's hat. As we walk along, we sometimes pick a sprig and stick it in a cap, for it will withstand the sun and heat, and still appear fresh when we return home to place it in a tiny golden vase.

A blue lupine carpet can give the most barren spot of earth the appearance of the sea, and as the eye feasts on its loveliness, there is a returning feeling of deep gratitude for the often-taken-for-granted beauty of this earth.

Lavishly the lupine appears and adapts itself to its given locality, more proof of the abundance of God's care for his children. Silently, the beauty comes to fruition while mankind is busy with many daily chores.

Then, when the walk is taken, the blue carpet is ready to delight. If the walk is delayed, some of the stalks already may be turning brown as the summer season begins.

In one difficult year, we almost missed the lupine entirely. Sickness and sorrow had kept us indoors, and when we went outside we were amazed to find the lupine on the hillside flinging a blanket of blue, as inviting as our bed had seemed in our weakness.

Now the strength of the lupine, returning for another spring, reminded of the resources of God which are available to those who go in search of them, asking in faith.

Prayer: God, we are grateful for all the reminders of thy beauty as seen in humble messengers such as the lupine. Keep us faithful. AMEN.

25 Wind Patterns

"Blessed is every one that feareth the Lord; that walketh in his ways."
PSALM 128:1

On a windy morning there is special zest in a good, brisk hike, but when the wind becomes too strong there is an element of fear attached to its blowing.

What will happen next? Will a branch blow down across the roof crashing into the shingles calling for extensive repair? Perhaps a window will be broken.

Inside, the blowing wind may seem even more dangerous than it does outside when one is taking giant strides to match the force of the wind.

If the wind comes from behind, it can blow a person onward so that time spent on the usual amount of trail is reduced, but it may be more than made up for when the return is attempted against the wind current.

In fact, if one's trail is along a modern freeway,

gasoline consumption may actually be cut if the wind is behind the car, and the mileage decreased when the car is forced to go against the wind.

When the wind finally subsides, there is always a change even on the well-worn paths. The experienced hiker learns to look for certain traces of the wind having been ahead of him.

Here will be a freshly swept stretch of sand, looking for all the world as if a zealous housewife had taken her broom and pushed away all debris, even large grains of sand and pebbles.

In another portion there will be a jagged cut across the trail where a large branch has been blown by the wind. The point where the twigs join the branch will be clearly marked in the wind pattern left on the trail.

A bit of bark will be blown directly in the center of the roadway. When picked up and examined, the hiker may find a different kind of tree or bush than he had thought was present in this area.

Sometimes the wind will return with a rush and without warning. It may reverse itself to a different direction. Perhaps the sage bushes will lean toward the east and not to the west as earlier in the day.

Constantly surrounding man, who is often unaware of these natural factors, is the shift of wind currents making different patterns on walkways as well as through the sky for aviators to watch and use.

Small wonder that man sometimes fears and is lonely, surrounded by such invisible powers. A blessing awaits when he fits his steps not to the wayward wind, but to the ways of the Lord, who alone is worthy to be feared.

Prayer: God, we are weary of the winds of chance in our lives. Help us claim the blessing of thy presence through each day. AMEN.

26 The Feeding Quail

"And it came to pass, that at even the quails came up, and covered the camp: and in the morning the dew lay round about the host." Exodus 16:13

Darting out from the underbrush at the side of the trail crossing directly in front of us, appeared a covey of quail. Mother and father were followed by four tiny quail, walking as fast as their little legs could carry them.

There is something unfailingly beautiful about the sight of a quail family in search of food together on the hillsides. Father and mother are like the king and queen of the western bird range.

No children are more carefully trained in the habits of their own kind than are the baby quail, who are miniature replicas of the regal adult birds.

Seeing them pass our walk always reminds of the story of the manna, which God provides for all his creatures, first described in the Old Testament.

We are told that "at even the quails came up, and covered the camp," this time a part of the provender for the children in the wilderness. At morning there was dew and manna.

In all the generations since, the quails themselves have been able to find manna in the western hills and plains, taking their families with them in search of the grain.

Sometimes they can be persuaded to come to homes for special hand-outs of grain. On our hilltop, they will come to the section which is still barren if we place grain for them.

As yet they refuse to come where the lawn is green. The reason for this baffles us, but we have learned to take a few extra steps to the brown hillside to leave the grain. Then, if we watch closely we will see the quail come to retrieve the grain and go back into the underbrush.

Sometimes on a routine day with a temptation to discouragement or worry, it is therapy to pick up a big handful of grain and go out to attract the quail.

They come to the table to accept what is offered them, eating with great dignity, and going serenely on their accustomed way, often taking their young with them.

From the quail feeding on our hillside we have learned anew the lesson of trusting God to provide daily manna, whether it comes from a job, a call from a friend, or a welcome letter.

Prayer: God, give us the manna we need in our hearts this day that we may be nourished, and sustained to serve thee better. AMEN.

27 Bouquet of Weeds

"The waters compassed me about, even to the soul: the depth closed me round about, the weeds were wrapped about my head." JONAH 2:5

Weeds by the side of the trail at first seemed in direct contrast to the flowers after we had learned to tell one plant from another.

One of the disturbing things about gardening, or hiking, is that it takes some real discernment to tell a flower from a weed. We have been conditioned to think that weeds automatically are ugly, and we know they can grow at great rates to choke the flowers.

No matter how diligently we try, some weeds always remain in the best-tended garden, and along trails where nobody is responsible for the weeding, the plants classified as weeds may grow in profuse abundance.

It is only when autumn comes that they are seen in a light different from the rest of the year when they are usually considered a pest. In autumn, one of the joys of a hike on a cool, crisp morning is the picking of a bouquet of weeds.

Then the green branches have turned brown, yellow, gold, and sometimes red. What seemed a scrawny green plume of leaves is now a miniature tree with autumn foliage when picked from the weed base and held aloft in the sunlight.

The tiny weeds which grow closer to the soil between the rocks also turn colors. In fact, when seen from the top of a hill looking downward across the soil in autumn, the weeds may give such a view of russet and burnt orange that they become in imagination a whole forest.

The effect is much like that of a good puppet performance when gradually the tiny figures grow in stature, so that at the end of the performance, it is a shock when the men or women who operate the miniature dolls are exposed.

Many are the delights of the weeds when seen at their best in autumn, my husband and I have discovered in our morning walks. We keep a tall vase in the kitchen which receives its weed bouquet early in October and it often lasts until time for the Christmas decorations to take its place.

We have learned to accept the weeds with as

good grace as possible, for all know what Jonah meant when he said "the weeds were wrapped about my head." Yes, weeds in the sea, weeds in the desert, or weeds in the heart abound. The trick is to find their beauty and not let them bind us to ugliness.

Prayer: God, keep us from littering our lives with habits which need to be weeded out, and help us take beauty from ugliness. AMEN.

28 The Forgotten Iris

"And in the morning, then ye shall see the glory of the Lord." EXODUS 16:7

Each morning is a fresh gift from the hand of the Lord, but sometimes this is forgotten through daily routine until a surprise makes the morning seem like a miracle.

And, so it was on the morning when we came face to face with the glory of the forgotten iris bed. For many weeks we had walked past a clump of greenery near a blackened spot of earth which indicated that, at some time, there had been a house or shed located nearby.

As is the way with nature, the grass had taken over the barren and burned spots. There were tangled areas where it was impossible to see the ground at all.

On this particular morning, we saw some lavender and purple with the green and went closer to see what was causing the contrast. There, in its infinite beauty, was a perfectly formed iris blossom, delicate as an exotic orchid.

We looked closer and saw many iris buds on the other tall green shoots. One flag was already unfurling to the sunlight, and was only one of a whole border of buds soon to bloom.

Then we knew there had indeed been a house here, and that at sometime past someone had planted a number of iris bulbs. Or had this border started with only one treasured gift bulb?

Over the years, the iris had multiplied and survived even without special care. Perhaps the rains of the past season had something to do with their flowering this particular spring.

We made it a special season of enjoyment as we walked past the iris for the next two weeks, feeling we had our own iris garden to enjoy day after day.

Who had planted the original iris? A housewife trying to beautify this rugged area which perhaps a prospector-husband had selected? Had the couple come to regain lost health, counting on the sunshine and quiet atmosphere to restore them to normal living?

The secret was well-kept with the purple iris. Silently we blessed the unknown keeper of the garden who had left such a legacy for others to enjoy as they passed by on their journeys.

The neglected iris showed us what we needed to remember, that we also have the opportunity of passing on beauty, truth, and integrity to generations yet to come, as they use our institutions. It is our privilege to preserve our heritage and plant other seeds of love and peace to flourish in future years.

Prayer: God, bless our churches and community organizations, and help us make our full contribution so the future may be blessed. AMEN.

94

29 Busy as Ants

> "Ye shall walk in all the ways which
> the Lord your God hath commanded
> you, that ye may live, and that it may
> be well with you, and that ye may
> prolong your days in the land which
> ye shall possess." DEUTERONOMY 5:
> 33

Encountering a long line of ants busy at work on
the trail, we thought at first that someone was un-
winding a spool of black thread. The line of in-
dustrious ants extended so far that we dared not
estimate their number in the hundreds or even
thousands.

Each followed his own prescribed routine, for
ants are superbly organized, and every ant seems
to know exactly which role to take in the great
drama of the ant organization.

Often what seem to be just a few ants going to a
hole in the ground with tiny crumbs will turn out
to be a long procession. It could extend to the op-
posite side of the trail, follow the underbrush for
a few feet, return to the trail to cross the walk, and

go to the other side where the food supplies are deemed best.

On one occasion we found the ants diligently digging into such hard red earth that we wondered how they could move any portion of it. Eventually they had their hole in the stiff earth, surrounded on each side by soft anthills where they had sifted the dirt into smooth even granules.

Again, we found them working an unlikely spot that they eventually abandoned. Unperturbed, the ants turned to another site, this time beside the beaten path. A bush had been pulled so that the soil near the roots was softer and easier for them to move.

This time the chain of command extended so far into the underbrush that we could not follow it to its end, but could only stand and admire the brisk industry which was taking food to the colony.

Something tells the busy ants what to do, when to do it, and how to accomplish their ends. It is a humbling sight to watch them follow through with such energy, going to a definite goal.

Too often in thinking of the ants, we remember only their busyness, how they keep working, and are not sluggards. What we need to remember is

that they are following a plan providing abundant-
ly for their very beings.

Surely the God who provides for the ants will
have a plan for all his human creatures who ask
for guidance through prayer and are willing to use
their energy to build successful projects.

Being busy is not enough. The ants follow the
plan meant for ants. As human beings there are
wonderful plans for each of our lives.

Prayer: God, keep us from wasteful busyness, and
help us know in our hearts exactly what we should
do to fulfill thy plans. AMEN.

30 Caw, Caw, Caw

"O house of Jacob, come ye, and let us walk in the light of the Lord."
Isaiah 2:5

From high on the telephone pole, at the end of the road leading to the dusty trail, came the sound caw, caw, caw. Immediately we looked up, and there was a crow, calling to us from his perch in the sky.

My husband turned to me and said, "Why do you suppose the crow is calling caw to us this particular morning? Is he just trying to sound friendly?"

We wondered if his call was to warn other birds that two human beings were coming into their natural territory. Then we speculated that perhaps he was just indulging in a form of vocal exercise.

But the crow persisted with his call until it began to sound like complaining at some irritation. Soon we stopped to look at him more closely, and at this

98

the complaining crow wanted us to admire his large wingspan.

Swiftly he lifted himself into the morning breeze and took himself with powerful strokes straight across the blue sky.

As he showed us his graceful flight due to his strong wings, we forgot his complaining voice and the way he had chided us. We put the strident sound of his chorus behind us and pondered the mystery and power of wings.

For centuries mankind tried to imitate wings until air power was developed. The biblical poets spoke of the morning itself as coming on wings. We sometimes speak of "wings of song."

These lovely phrases are just reflections of an even more cherished flight, that which happens when we as individuals learn to trust our own wings enough to fly through life on the steady beats of hope, trust, and faith.

Often we remain sitting on the nearest bench or chair bleating a complaining caw, caw, caw to anyone who will listen. What we need to do is launch our own wings of talent and see how far we can fly into areas of service.

From Old Testament times this has been the wistful invitation of God to his children, asking them to "walk in the light of the Lord." Such a walk calls for putting complaints aside and having trust in the stalwart wings of prayer.

Prayer: God, give us the faith we need to test our wings, and the wisdom to stop our plaintive cries of complaining. AMEN.

31 The Lost Gull

*"If I take the wings of the morning,
and dwell in the uttermost parts of
the sea; Even there shall thy hand
lead me, and thy right hand shall hold
me."* PSALM 139:9, 10

In the hush before the rainstorm, the gulls flew inward, coming to the area where we hike, flapping their wings in the sky above us.

Even as we hurried home to escape the heavy showers, the gulls were circling overhead as if trying to decide which way to the safest haven.

Not often do the birds from the ocean come this far inland, so we were not surprised when the rainfall was unusually heavy and lasted more days than normal.

The gulls had warned us, for they were creatures of the sea and had their own built-in knowledge of the storms, knowledge which sometimes baffles mankind.

Yet man is promised that even if he goes to the "uttermost parts of the sea," God is there with his wisdom and the protection of his right hand. Many sailors have believed in this beautiful verse, and many lonely hearts have turned to it in hours of deep discouragement on land.

Often life is filled with uncertain, troubled seas, and we need to be reminded of the presence of God in such stormy situations. Seeing the flight of the gulls is reassurance of this precious promise.

It was disconcerting to find that when the flock had moved onward, there remained one little lost gull. We first saw him at the bird bath and thought he might have been watching us as we walked home from the muddy trail.

The gull was too shy to come to the water in the shallow trough until all land birds had left. Then he flew cautiously and paused on the rim, as if wondering why the water was so still, not moving like the waves of his familiar ocean.

Obviously he was hungry, but he was timid about accepting food from the feeding ground if any other birds were around. When he had eaten his fill, he took to sudden flight as if to try to catch up with the vanished flock.

He moved swiftly away, gliding over the valley much as other gulls we had watched in the wake of our freighter when going around the world.

102

We wished godspeed to the little lost gull and marveled at the inner knowledge he possessed of where to find food and water for the journey. He left us with a new appreciation of the God who cares for his creatures, even to the uttermost parts of the sea.

Prayer: God, we lift our hands to thee, and ask for thy tender support of us in the shifting storms of our lives. AMEN.

32 Tarantula Appears

> *"He that walketh uprightly walketh surely: but he that perverteth his ways shall be known."* PROVERBS 10:9

The tarantula was walking along with great speed when we first spied him on the dusty trail ahead of us. True, his gait was angular and he looked a bit awkward, but he was making wonderful time on his spider-like legs.

We stopped to count them, having to lean forward a bit to keep in time with his rhythmic walk, but we determined that he had eight legs plus two feelers.

All were attached to a body which looked like a form of chenille bedspread material, so we dubbed him at once Fuzzy Wuzzy and took a better look at this seldom-seen tarantula of the western hillsides.

He had appeared so self-confident swinging down the trail, that at first he did not realize that he was being watched. Apparently when this realization trickled through to him, he changed his route at once.

With his quick step forward, he crouched down as if he wanted to make himself small so we would not be able to see him. In this position he looked as if he were headed backwards. We couldn't see his eyes, but only from the direction the feelers were pointed could we tell in what direction Fuzzy Wuzzy was headed.

How frightened he looked, when it is usually the other way around, for the tarantula is feared by hikers, perhaps because of the stories told of his ferocity. He always looks as though he might be a trail menace.

But when we stopped to take a good look at him, we saw the delicate colorations of his fuzzy body and the sharp contrast of the sturdy legs which carry him over small stones which must seem like boulders to him as he feels his way.

Only when his fear stopped him did he seem to cringe and be less than the unusual, interesting creature that he had been made. When he had been walking confidently, he made steady progress toward his destination.

Often fear can pervert the way of any creature and change him into something which cringes and pauses, unable to move in either direction. Such perversion is to be avoided at all costs, and the remedy is confidence in God's goodness and a willing acceptance of those met along life's trail.

Prayer: Father, if fear keeps us from reaching out to those we see each day, give us new strength to walk uprightly with confidence. AMEN.

33 Insidious Termites

> *"To give light to them that sit in darkness and in the shadow of death, to guide our feet into the way of peace."* LUKE 2:79

One of the most memorable mornings of our hiking appeared by usual standards to be just an ordinary day until we came upon the colony of termites.

They had covered their trail so well that we had walked past them many mornings, unaware of their busy and insidious presence. This morning we paused for a moment and idly kicked at a log by the side of the trail.

Instantly the wood came to life; then it seemed to disintegrate as the countless tiny termites moved away from it in great confusion because of the light. They must work in the dark because they perish in the light.

Apparently for some time they had been intent on destroying the log so they could use it for food. They had covered the brown wood until it looked like a chocolate log from the deposits of the mucilage-like substance from their bodies mixed with dark earth.

Busy in the dark, hidden from the light, they had almost destroyed this firm log. Sometimes their industry causes great harm to residences, churches, or valuable pieces of furniture.

The worst part of termite destruction is that it is already accomplished before the individual learns of the havoc which has been made in the darkness. Unfortunately this is often true in hearts and homes as well.

The sins which are kept in the dark grow and destroy such valuables as love and honor until there is a great crumbling of respect and integrity.

Perhaps a cherished marriage has been destroyed, or a child is involved with drugs, before the insidious sins committed in darkness are known.

When brought under the healing light of God's love, such sins can die as the termites perish when exposed to light. If they find a way to return to the dark, they continue eating the wood from the inside, and prosper again.

The individual who wants to walk "into the way

of peace" needs friends who care enough to shield him from returning to sinful haunts and practices in his environment.

Termites are limited to working in the dark by their very natures. Man is made in the image of God and so has the blessed ability to come out of darkness to walk peacefully in the warmth of God's healing light.

Prayer: God, help us to live in the light of thy great love, safely removed from the limiting powers of darkness. AMEN.

34 The Unmoved Trail

"Yea, though I walk through the valley of the shadow of death, I will fear no evil: for thou art with me; thy rod and thy staff they comfort me."
PSALM 23:4

Sometimes it is hard to remember that the trail is still there when life becomes full of many other things, especially stress and sorrow. Once, after weeks laden with various problems, we realized we had been neglectful of the daily walk. Even though the walk had been taken physically, our minds had been occupied with other details, so we had forgotten the beauty of the morning and the joy of trail experiences.

Yet there came a special day of sunshine when we took a good look at the old trail and realized that it was indeed there where it had always been. Life with the insects, flowers, grass, birds, and clouds overhead had gone on serenely without us.

We had changed inside and had been oblivious to what had remained as usual—the good earth with trails to walk in the morning sunlight.

It was a reassuring moment of coming to a new plateau in the climb which the heart takes through life. We knew we must get back to the feel of the trail, and how good the ground seemed now beneath our feet!

A solid trail, unmoved by circumstances, is one of the blessings which the hiker needs but so often takes for granted. Trails usually do not move from their accustomed spots, and are there for us to find again after sorrow and strain.

If a great storm washes out a mountain trail, some evidences of the road usually remain, and the first attempt is to restore the path to its former condition. Sometimes a slight change must be made in contour if the new roadway is to serve the purpose of taking the traveler to his destination.

Different shadows may fall on the trail because of the nearby trees or the stark skeletons of tall bushes. Things may look quite different in a season of sorrow than one of gladness.

It always remains important to get back to the trail and walk again in familiar pathways, meeting people in ordinary places who want to help us through our changing experiences.

Friends, family, club members, and church

groups are important in life's journey. Sooner or later all of us have reason to be glad for the un-moved trail to which we may return.

Prayer: God, we thank thee for all evidences of thy permanence as we walk life's changing pathways of joy and sorrow. Amen.

35 Alive with Life

"I will walk before the Lord in the land of the living." PSALM 116:9

As we started on the trail my husband said, "Everything looks so alive this morning."

It was true, for the fresh green grass had followed the rain. Parts of the brown hillside, which had been barren for several seasons, now seemed planted with new crops greening in the golden sunlight.

The birds sounded blithe and happy, almost noisy because of the abundance of their joyful songs. One flew overhead, circling us, and in the bright light we could see the tiny throat quiver. We marveled at how so much harmonious music could come tumbling from so small an area.

As we rounded a turn on the trail we found a new bed of flowers and were reminded that a year ago we had seen this same cluster of purple and white blossoms close to the ground lifting their

113

chalices to the sky. This miniature garden had suddenly come into bloom again as a part of the living pattern of life.

A few feet further we came upon even more conclusive proof that the scene was surging with life. The ancient yet ageless cactus plants which had seemed so flat and lifeless, were now thick and bulging with juice.

Their stored-up, life-giving waters were turning the gray shades of the succulent branches to a fresher color of gray-green. Already there was promise of colorful blossoms, the desert "orchids" which provide so much loveliness in alien soil.

At the top of a small hill we paused to look around at all the fresh evidences of new life and to be grateful for this moment of awareness. We remembered the vow of the psalmist who said, "I will walk before the Lord in the land of the living."

It was a time to leave death and sorrow as far behind as we could put them, a moment of common humanity. We remembered also that this same psalm of life contains a very pertinent verse, "I love the Lord, because he hath heard my voice and my supplications."

From God comes the comfort to accept the new-

114

ness of life even though it must be lived without the support and consolation of those who have been held most dear and who have given meaning to life.

Each spring on earthly trails, there is an eternal reminder that God is the God of the living and constantly renews and refreshes. It is ours to decide to walk as cheerfully as possible in this land of the living.

Prayer: God of all comfort, renew within us a proper spirit so our daily walk may be alive with the life which comes from thee. AMEN.

36 Crossroad Bunnies

> *"And Achish said, Whither have ye made a road today? And David said, Against the south of Judah, and against the south of the Jerahmelites, and against the south of the Kenites."*
> I SAMUEL 27:10

At first we could not decide what had made the little crossroads which we saw verging from our main trail. As the season progressed, these paths seemed to grow a little wider and deeper.

It seemed incredible that tiny footprints of birds or animals could indeed make such a visible pathway among the weeds and over the sand and pebbles. Could one of the roadmakers be the roadrunner who walks with such a swift angular gait?

Invisible feet might have been making the roads for all we knew, for we could not catch any trail creature in the act. Then, as we changed the time of the morning walk to an earlier hour because of the summer heat, the mystery became clear.

The many crossroads were made by the bunnies of our area in search of food. Sometimes, in the early morning hours, they would sit on our wider trail, watching us in friendly fashion. Their tall ears seemed to be listening, and their sharp eyes watched intently.

After they had come to know us as regulars on the early morning trail, they would not move out of the way until we got within a few feet of them. Then they would scurry from the main trail and lope over some of the crossroads we had been wondering about and watching as we walked.

From the top of our hilltop resting place at the halfway point of our hike, we could get an excellent view of the many trails which had been forged by the bunnies in their years of foraging.

We found them excellent highway engineers, for the crisscrossing trails looked like highway interchanges at points where the trails met after long stretches of straight paths.

We marveled that their soft feet could form such solid, well-defined trails, little by little, day after day, year after year. We enjoyed watching them as they sped down the trails, their white powder puff tails bobbing up and down with each scampering step.

As we watched, we were imprinting our own

morning trails by walking. Automatically each of us makes our own life's trail through daily habits.

Over the years that trail grows more pronounced and visible, whether a route of selfishness or service.

Prayer: God, help us so to live that we may have a ready answer when questioned about the roads of service our lives build. AMEN.

37 Fox Puppies at Play

"Surely the mountains bring him forth food, where all the beasts of the field play." **Job 40:20**

Dashing across the trail in front of us near the curve ahead we saw two bits of red fluff. Soon they zipped back across the path, the one in back apparently trying to catch the swishing bushy tail of the leader.

As we wondered how to identify the playmates, we heard a rustle at the side of the trail and stopped still, almost on tiptoe. Peering at us from under a mesquite bush was a red fox puppy, and obviously we were the first human beings he had ever seen at close range. His curiosity exceeded our delight.

Almost instantly the second puppy appeared, his head cocked at an interesting angle. Both continued to study us as if we had just arrived from another planet, and indeed we were foreign to their home territory.

119

Then with a quick movement they both disappeared in the underbrush, almost like two small children playing tag with each other, or hide-and-seek from grown-ups.

A moment later we saw a larger bushy tail over the sage bush and heard a sharp yelp. Obviously the mother fox had found them and corralled them to give them a good cuff and keep them from playing with strangers.

By now we realized they must belong to the magnificent fox we had seen at our bird bath when we awakened early one very hot morning a week or so ago.

Father fox had jumped into the cool water with his front paws, lowered his head with his pointed nose down to the water, and had drunk his fill. Then he had jumped down in one quickly graceful motion, leaving his wet pawprints on our patio cement.

He had loped off, probably to join these very pups who were now playing in the brush along the roadside trail. We were destined to see them again on two other mornings, chasing each other so gaily we could almost hear their laughter or animal giggles.

Always the antics of the playful fox pups, running in such carefree abandon, returns as a happy relaxing moment. Play is instinctive with almost all young animals, including the children in our homes.

Somewhere along life's path, many of us lose the ability to relax at will in spontaneous play. The playful moment is to be cultivated as an antidote for work or weariness and is a firm base on which to build more successful activity.

Prayer: God, help us to remain children at heart, and to keep happy hearts for full enjoyment of both play and work. AMEN.

38 Wise Squirrels

> *"Then said the Lord unto Moses, Behold, I will rain bread from heaven for you; and the people shall go out and gather a certain rate every day, that I may prove them, whether they will walk in my law, or no."* Exodus 16:4

Starting on the trail in sturdy walking shoes is always an adventure, for we never know which animals or birds we shall find looking for their day's food. Will it be the pretty sparrow, the one which wears such a jaunty little white hat?

One morning we glimpsed a tiny gray animal ahead of us and hoped so much it was not a helpless, tame kitten, abandoned here to fend for itself in the wilds.

Then we heard a warning screech and knew it was a mother squirrel calling out to warn her young not to come near.

She stood near a woodpile, for over the years tree branches had been piled at this particular spot of the trail. We had secured our own walking sticks from here when we first began to hike.

Now much of the wood was weathered like drift-wood from the sea, and the soft gray bark would make an ideal home for the baby squirrels.

Mother squirrel seemed frozen to the spot, hoping we would not see her, but we outwaited her till she finally found courage to run and leap into the woodpile. A few mornings later we saw the frisky baby squirrels sunning themselves and darting beneath branches.

No doubt mother was away, again filling her cheeks and her front paws with natural riches. Squirrels are wise enough to secure much food while it is available and to store it away and use it when necessary.

Next season they refill their squirrel pantries, or animal bank accounts. In this they show a wisdom often forgotten by those who hike the trails.

Often people, who have had cause to be thrifty and store their means, fail to learn how to enjoy their substance in later times. Waiting for the rainy day often keeps us from seeing today's sunshine.

Getting and keeping often become the whole rule, instead of only a part of it. The second part calls for using and sharing. Then the energies are freed for tackling new goals of work and finance in the changing season.

The wise squirrels search, store, and share their food. Then they are ready with strength to enjoy the new season in God's good time and providence.

Prayer: God, keep us from hoarding our funds and our happiness. Let us be generous in spirit as we share in thy goodness. AMEN.

39 Walking Memory's Trail

> "*Set thee up waymarks, make thee high heaps: set thine heart toward the highway, even the way which thou wentest.*" JEREMIAH 31:21

One morning, as silently we walked the trail near our home, my husband suddenly remarked, "Such a lot of trails to remember." Instantly I thought of the yellow wild flowers by the white sands near the blue waters of the Sea of Galilee.

Then there was the afternoon we had parked our car along the Alcan Highway just to take a walk and stretch our legs, and each passing car stopped in neighborliness to offer help.

The sweet scent of lemon as we walked along the Riviera watching the ocean by moonlight returned now in lovely fragrant remembrance, as did the flowering trees of the capitol city of Australia.

Walking memory's trails can be one of the joys of a lifetime, and indeed may be the only way to walk at life's ending, as a friend in a convalescent home reminded us recently.

Such memories do not just happen, but are the by-product of some project or activity. It is possible to daydream about many things and have a form of false happiness, but a memory must be experienced first as a living reality.

In the Old Testament, the prophets warned that the people should set up "waymarks" such as the signposts found on mountain trails. Told to make "high heaps" similar to the marking stones by the path, they were being encouraged to pile up deeds of unselfishness by which their paths of service could be plainly seen.

When the heart is set "toward the highway" of a goal, in moving forward it makes an enjoyable path on which to return when the mind can only take the journey in memory.

Always we are reminded of "the way which thou wentest," as the archaic language describes life's daily walk. That way might have included happy family memories of home and children, the vital enjoyment of a craft or profession, moments alone under the stars, or fellowship with neighbors and friends.

Often there is fresh strength for the ongoing journey in thinking of happy walks with friends now gone, who added their influence to our lives through the changing years.

Walking memory's trail need not be a lonely experience for the Bible gives a precious promise: "Lo, I am with you alway, even unto the end of the world" (Matthew 28:20).

There can be peace in the heart recalling life's trails walked in joy and in sorrow with Christ as a companion on the daily path.

Prayer: Dear God, help us walk wisely that the trail of memory may be blessed by thy hallowed presence always. AMEN.